Like Stars Across
My Skin

T.J. Zook

ISBN: 1723545961
ISBN-13: 978-1723545962

DEDICATION

Jaci, this one's for you. This piece of my soul
happened completely because you believed in me.
Thank you for acting as if I've already made it.

And to my editor, Lily, thank you. You deserve the
entire world. I literally (and I mean literally) could not
have done this without you.

CONTENTS

LETTER TO THE READER

By purchasing this book you are making a contribution to LitWorld, an organization that recognizes the barriers that children, both nationally and internationally, have in terms of access to literacy and aim to bridge that gap. I chose this foundation to donate to because LitWorld places an emphasis on being able to read and write as a means of telling one's story. I believe in the fundamental human right of having access to reading and writing materials, but more importantly, I believe that having that access means nothing if it is not an avenue to letting others hear of your own peril, plight, journey, and redemption. Children are actively writing the future, and this small gesture is me saying "I believe in you." I have been privileged enough to have access to an education that has enabled me to learn reading, writing, and story-telling techniques so that I may share on paper the things I have seen and grown through. This is me (and all of you) giving a little bit of that back.

Thank you.

This is the first book I have published as an openly bisexual woman. That might disappoint some of you, but this moment in my life is about being unapologetically truthful of who I am, in whatever capacity that is. Even if it's strange. Even if it doesn't add up. Even if I am uncomfortable. This book will also highlight my feelings for Jesus, because I am battling with all that I know of Christianity, and whether or not I believe what everyone has always taught me about God is true. I am still attempting to find some kind of middle ground between those two things (if one exists) and what that means for me.

There are two significant realizations that I have come to since starting the writing process with this book. The first is this: I have cared about everyone I ever have so passionately and beautifully. I pray that I never lose that about myself. I am not sorry for writing poems about love and loss time and time again, because this is my truth. This is the season I am in. So many people have convoluted ideas about women and how they should behave and think. We are so often seen as too emotional. I used to be so ashamed of feeling so much because I didn't want to be "that girl." I know now that feeling so much comes with being so much, and that there is nothing to be ashamed of. I would not trade that for the whole world.

The second realization I have come to is that I am happy for the first time in my life at twenty-four years old. The only theme throughout this whole book, throughout my whole life, is that I have always wanted what I convinced myself I would never get. Stability. Love. Freedom. Gentleness. It is for no reason other than protection, knowing that if I invest myself in something that will never want me back that I have no chance of letting anyone other than myself hurt me. I don't know if I'm more petrified that things will work out or that they won't. I cannot stomach the idea of someone loving me the right way because that means that all my cards are on the table.

My anxiety helps me screw up a lot of good things that come to me, whether it be relationships, friendships, jobs, what have you. I throw it all to the flames so that I have the right to say that I chose the outcome. I am choosing now to not allow that to be my reality anymore. I refuse to accept sadness, bitterness or misery as something that happens to someone without choice. It is for my own well-being that I will only allow those feelings to be things I have given permission to. I am also learning every single day that if at the end of my life the only person I can say I was ever in love with was myself, then I have won.

I don't mean that to say I have never had happy moments, or that I have never been joyful before. What I mean is that I finally, for the first time, feel secure. I feel beautiful. I feel capable. I am doing the right things for the first time and that is making me HAPPY. I feel at peace. I am no longer constantly scared because whether or not unfortunate things happen ultimately does not affect my peace. I have accepted the reality that things do not happen to me, they just happen. No one is waiting with a pitchfork and a torch outside my door. No one is purposefully creating misery in my life. Once I started assigning worth to myself and not settling for less than I want or deserve, I became a happier, kinder, softer, and better person. None of you will ever understand how many tears of joy I have cried because of that.

I put this book out there both as an act of sheer courage and as one of solidarity. One of the things I value the absolute most about myself is my transparency. I never want people to guess. I want to bare my naked soul 100 percent of the time.

I don't want to be famous. I don't want notoriety. I want to be exactly who I am in whatever capacity that may be. I do not have everything figured out yet. I am not completely healed. I have just learned that I am complete with or without the cracks.

Thank you so much for sharing this wor[l]d with me.

I don't really believe in astrology. I don't think so, at least. I have, however, taken to learning as much as I can about it. For example, I know that I am a Leo sun, Gemini moon, and Libra rising. I am told that those are fire and air signs which are inherently compatible, so my chart is not all over the place. My emotions, however, are. I am also told that I am a Virgo Venus, so my standards for partners are obnoxiously high. So far, nothing in the "love" department has worked out for long but I remain hopeful. Astrology is a fun topic of conversation and I have to admit that it is kind of nice to have something to blame my bad traits on. I also really dig outer space and making lists. Which is why I keep talking about it.

I am something of a flight risk, which I hear is typical of people with charts like mine. Never staying in one place or with one person long. Apparently, I am likely to be loyal to the core, but flighty. Reckless. Irresponsible. I end things before they get too serious. Leos are too proud to admit that they want to be adored so they go through a series of flirting and empty promises then abandon the whole thing. I like to start fights and pretend I'm the victim when I get "left," but really I had it planned all along so I could kill it before it killed me. These are not my finest traits. I wouldn't know what love was if it hit me in the face with a bat. I wonder if these traits would change if my chart were different. Probably not, because I don't believe in astrology.

I categorize everyone I run across in life by their star sign. Not for any reason other than my being a type A personality and that's an easy way for me to file-folder everyone. They come into my life, fleeting, like a shooting star. They leave my life the same way, blowing through the core of me when I take off like a rover looking for my next galaxy. After I am gone, I am never the same. The scars they leave look like stars across my skin. For moments at a time, I exist with constellations all around me.

ARIES

I cried while you were driving away because I knew I had to say goodbye. I knew that when you were gone, that was the last I would ever see of you.

I was scared knowing that my whole world was going to change.

I had spent the last 4 years befriending you and to think that I knew without a doubt that it was over with? That's what I cried for. I cried knowing that in a week we would no longer be on speaking terms.

I cried because you did not deserve it.

Did I Lose My Only Chance?

Nobody loved me as well as you did. Nobody was ever as good or as kind. Nobody else has ever been willing to give me the world like you were. I did not deserve a single second of your time. If there is anyone who I never should have had a chance with, it was you. You did not deserve me leaving you for someone who treated me so badly. You did not deserve the back and forth feelings. You did not deserve for me to lie about being in love with you. I am so sorry. Every single thing about it was my fault and not a single second of the bad times had anything to do with you. I remember you so fondly.

[1/1 ARIES HAVE LEFT THE CHAT]

TAURUS

I crave your still breath
Silence in moments
Where we fall in love
Just existing together

I am just waiting for the day
I develop
Enough bravery
To beg you

Run away with me

eyeroll

I missed your warm hands
Your passenger's seat
The way you'd smile when you'd look over at me
The talks that I never thought were long enough
I missed the tiny lisp when you'd talk
You took off running because you couldn't stand
Somebody loving you
You were never a man

That's why it only took me three days to move on
Men ain't shit

You were a stop sign I blew right through
Like a cop having a bad day
Reality got my ass for speeding
You were not worth this ticket

Kissing you was like a shotgun joyride
headed straight to hell
Missing you was like my favorite novel
with the ending ripped out

[2/2 TAURUS HAVE LEFT THE CHAT]

GEMINI

I'm drinking without you
This is the first time I've had to
Do I even like you when I'm sober?
Does this silence mean that we are over?

When most people kiss me it is hungry
Ravenous, vapid, empty
It's almost as if I am a meal they wish to devour
Like they have something to prove
By kissing me hard and passionate
That is usually the last I see of them

But you
With your twisted Gemini mind games
When you kiss me
It is timid and sweet
Like a teenager with a crush
Or the first time in a long time
You are slow and specific
Never pushing or expecting anything from me
Tender, like you want to protect me
While simultaneously fixing yourself
There is trepidation
Your hands shake a little bit
You never take it too far
Because you are taking it slow
You say I am worth savoring

You terrify me

I have been someone's savior before
And I have been someone's second choice
I love myself (and you) too much to do that again

I adore you
And I want the absolute best for you in life
But I can't be the only one of us that does

My mind is made up
I never meant to hurt you

I'm so sorry

You were a changing of the seasons
Too far in the past to see forward
I was a little girl lost with the worst intentions

You were my midnight fairytale
I was pushing you toward self-fulfillment
That you didn't want any part of

You were the waves, I was your summer
Beneath my heat, you fell under

I wish I could say you were my day
My night, my dusk and my dawn
I wish I had more to tell you

It was lengthy and dismissive
It was painful and corrupt
Everything I thought I wanted
Everything you knew you did

"If you will be my summers,
I will forever be your waves
You can be my submissive night,
I'll be your loyal days"

Much like the levees in a hurricane
Beneath your storms, I cracked
Releasing too much energy

The people around you were carried under
They had no choice but to submerge
I still mourn those innocent people

They needed their light but you burned me out
You were just longing waves
Now trampled with doubt

My adoration for you was the tides reeled in
With every word you said
They moved closer to the shore
What happened next no one could predict
You were the waves and the day
With no night or escape

What happened to me then
Could have never been seen
The season of summer disappeared into your dreams

I still have the memories
Though I no longer have tides
I vanished like the smoke of the summer

I get it, I get it
You called me flighty
And you were right
I guess that means you should have seen this coming

I was your nights, but I was also your days
It all now encircles me in a purple smoke haze

I was your summer, you were my waves
You were enthralled in the most overt of ways
Now the memory of me is all that remains

[1/1 LEO HAS LEFT THE CHAT]

CANCER

Loving you and losing you were the two hardest things I have ever had to do in my life. You were my all in, bets off, hands cuffed, end-all, be-all. Looking back now, that's exactly why I had to hand you over to fate. I'm not happy I had my heart ripped out of an open mouth but I know it was everything I needed.

That's the issue, I think, is that I never gave you up. I never handed you over to fate, to God, to whatever took you. You were removed from my hands and I was so unwilling to let you go that now you have claw marks all over you. If you came back you wouldn't be what you were before, what I loved so dearly. You'd be the mangled mess of what I didn't know how to let go of gracefully. I am so sorry.

There are things I like now that I didn't like before you like honey mustard and conflict resolution.

I sometimes go to Sonic and order a vanilla cream sweet tea and think about how bad it must be for me and how bad I must have been for you. I wonder where you are and how you're doing and if you ever think of me when you get vanilla cream sweet tea.

People like me better now than they did before you. You taught me how to lose my temper and adopt a kindness. Before you, I was hateful and rude and cruel. These days I'm pretty easy to get along with.

But you couldn't.
That's valid and I support it even if I don't understand it because I love you.
Loved you.
Whichever.

I had a dream about you last night and now I need you to know I forgive you for all of it. For coming, for going, for leaving me heartbroken.

Sometimes people don't stick around and the relationship is beautiful in spite of it. I value autonomy. So I have to value yours too.

For a little while during you, I stopped being jaded and let people in. I trusted my own feelings and connections and let them guide me. Now I cannot handle anyone having that kind of ammo. I would rather myself ruin everything at the beginning because then I at least have myself to blame. I know I only have myself to blame.

Now you're six months gone and I'm still hands-stretched-out reaching for you, hoping you'll find your way back into me through a glitch in the universe's fabric.

I've learned not to need you, though.
I've learned who I am.
That I am enough.
You were always the better part of me.
I am now the best part of myself.

I've seen people leave before you but none of them made me realize how fleeting human relationships are. How love is not always forever. How love is good even when it isn't forever. How you never had to stay forever for me to have loved you as much as a human possibly could.
And I do.
I always will.

You taught me how to do that. How to love and let go. How to love even if it hurts and that it's okay to love someone who isn't in your life anymore.

I guess this is where I let go of you. At the end of me. Rolling out of my body and off of my fingertips and into the big empty void that is eternity. I hear you drop to the bottom of the puddle at my feet. And with that noise, the end of "we."

There are things I like now that I didn't before you like honey mustard

and myself.

I don't always do the right thing but I usually do the kind thing and I want to thank you so much for teaching that to me. It may not have been so pretty while it was ending but my goodness it was so beautiful while we had it. I don't talk to God much these days but when I do I say "thank you thank you thank you for letting me experience that."

To this day I would trust you to make the best decision in regards to my well-being. I have trusted you with my life since the day I met you, kind and informed Cancer girl. You would never in your life make a decision out of spite or cruelty with me. I sometimes wish I were more like that with myself but I'm glad you taught me how to be that way with others.

I remember you sweetly
At a rest stop right outside of the city
On my last day where you brought me
We took pictures at sunset behind the trees

It is one of my favorite memories
That I will keep with me always

Piece By Piece

I will build a family
Kinder and more simple

I will build a family
Stronger and less fickle

I will build a family
Full of love and full of grace

I will build a family
Never worried if I will stay

I will build a family
Who are happy but not perfect

I will build a family
Who talk through every conflict

I will build a family
Who value wisdom and maturity

I will build a family
Who have safety and security

I will build a family
And the family will build me

I will raise a daughter
Who gets everything she needs

The first time you go on a Tinder date that turns into a "hit it and quit it," scenario, it's going to fuck you up pretty badly.

See, the great banter is going to get you. Maybe a little fast, but you like where it's headed. The first date is so sweet and someone actually kissed you first, which has you a little taken aback. You're going to ask yourself a million times "is this the right thing to do? Should I let them stay over? Maybe their intentions are good. What if their intentions aren't good?" Then you're going to do it anyway. And you're going to know right away the next morning that it's over. It's going to hit you like a ton of bricks that you just gave a stranger access to your body. How could you hurt yourself like that?

The first time you are a "hit it and quit it," it's going to feel a lot like wasps. They're all over your body and you can't swat them off and running would only make things worse. And you can't walk outside because you can't move because of the wasps and everything is closing in on you and it's all too much. Why do you feel like you are you in this alone? Does everything feel this lonely when you can't trust yourself anymore? Who is the person sitting inside your skin stealing the warmth from your bones? Get out of my body, who let you in here?!

Then you're going to realize it's you, just hollowed out, sitting in there. It's you, but with your knees to your chest, terrified, backed into a corner. After you get hit with "this is going too fast, I'm not ready for a relationship," over text message, it's going to feel like you stabbed yourself in your own back with a rusty bent kitchen knife. You're going to feel like you let yourself down and the sheer amount betrayal will bring you to your knees. It's going to make your stomach turn.

You are polite about it when you text them back. You're not going to go all "psycho girlfriend" on anyone because you've been working on this thing where you are kind without reason. You'll wish them the best even though you're furious and disappointed and sad and disgusted with yourself. You let your guard down and it turned out exactly how you didn't want it to. You handed someone the privilege of having you and they didn't cherish it like you swore the next person would. There's no amount of times you can wash your sheets or pillowcases or the clothes you wore that night to take that back. You're going to look for yourself under the bed, in the closet, behind the sofa, because the person you've grown into is hiding. You want to tell her "come back into me, my sweet. It is warm in here and I am empty without you. I will protect you, I promise" and she will not believe you. Would you believe you? All that work you've done on yourself in the past year is going to seem meaningless.

The first time you are a "hit it and quit it," you're going to cry a lot. It's not because you can't seem to find love, so something must be wrong with you. It's also not because you made a horrible mistake and you can't take it back. No, instead, you're going to cry as hard and as much as you can so that you may start regenerating new cells. The absolute stranger that was in your bed doesn't get to take anything with them if you make yourself new. These are growth tears.

You're going to cry because when you were kind to them and wished them the best, you meant it. How beautiful is it that you have grown into that person? That someone, someday, will love that about you? You're going to cry and you're going to become. You're going to cry and then your boss is going to promote you and describe you to his peers as "wildly optimistic," when nobody 5 years ago would have ever. Then you're going to make your first friend in a big city, her name is Chelsea and she sees you for who you are. The tears are going to become forgiveness fountains you are extending to yourself because maybe you're flawed, but you're also redeemed.

The first time you are a "hit it and quit it," will be the last. You know that now. Maybe it was not a part of your initial plan, but what is beauty if not reformed brokenness?

Cancer Cusp

Tears in your eyes you said to me
"I love you, I have always loved you
I just can't shake it"
Me? I didn't say anything at all
I knew what I was doing
When I flirted with you
You knew, too

"Be tender," you whispered to me softly
Nervous fingers, sweaty palms
Refusing direct eye contact
"Yes, I love you"
Tears now running down
Your rose-red cheeks
"But you're leaving
You are always leaving"

"Hi, I'm _____"

Just like the leaves in the Pacific Northwest autumn

I fall
I fall
I fall for you

Venus in Retrograde

I recall now a connection I made
While Venus was still in retrograde
Through the years my writing has matured in style
But something about her awakened my inner child

The end of Libra season was drawing near
I had a night job at a hotel serving beer
At the time, that was my repertoire
Then she came and sat at the end of my bar

"With a twist," she asked of her gin martini
As she swooned over a podcast duo she was seeing
A rush of blood to my cheeks, now beet red
I was hanging on every word she said

I was enchanted before she even said "hey"
Then she proceeded to tell me her name
"It's with two L's, spelled the right way"
Is she even real? I was in a daze

I fumbled over my words when I'm normally smooth
She said goodbye to me after she finished her food
I thought "it would be great to take her on a date"
But she left for the night and it was too late

"Please don't be in love with someone else"
I had Taylor Swift playing in my head to myself
It was fleeting and wonderful and all so brand new
"Please don't have somebody waiting on you"

We met again when the recording was over
Magnificent, she was wearing this glow about her
"Were they great?" I asked, with a grin as an answer
I had never in my life been so charmed by a Cancer

It jarred me to meet someone whose lips spill passion
Smoother than whiskey in an Old Fashioned
It seemed like it was us against the clock
I would have spent forever listening to her talk

And it's so strange because within moments I knew
She was someone I'd compare everyone else to
I hoped upon hope that was not the end
I still dream all the time I'll run into her again

I let the opportunity slip through my fingers
When she had to go and time couldn't linger
It was just a matter of picking the right words to say
I didn't muster up the confidence to be a bit brave

But if a glitch in space or a fault in time
Should ever bring her world back into mine
By whatever change in tide or phase of the moon
I pray the moment not be gone so soon

My little heart now - oh it is tethered
To a smirk on a face may I always remember
Tied to bangs and blue eyes somewhere in Idaho
Well wishes now wherever she goes

Be patient with me, please, I am begging you. I have never wanted to not fuck something up so badly in my life.

One look at you and I thought,

So this is it.
This is how galaxies are formed.

[4/5 CANCERS HAVE LEFT THE CHAT]

LEO

I sometimes recognize myself more
in my shadow
than I do in my reflection

[1/4]

Suit of armor, sword at the ready. She marched up the stairs lined with fire, ready to battle the beast that had spent decades terrorizing her city. Sure, maybe she was the princess of her kingdom, but that did not mean she would not be a fierce and brave warrior. Fervor and determination were set deep within her if for no reason other than out of pure spite for those who said she could not do it. Exhausted, she fell to her knees after reaching the landing at the top of the tower. Just before attempting to pull her self up, the princess sensed something eerie that sent her heart dropping to the pits of her stomach. She opened the door just a tiny bit, peeped through, and covered her mouth to mask the noise from a horrified gasp.

Everything is so loud in my head
    like pots and pans clanging
or like a full marching band
    but nothing is louder than pressurized silence
that pushes against the sides
    it's violence
and makes me want to die
    oh my god I want to die

There is nothing more terrifying and lonely than being under the impression that you are making yourself scarce when you are the elephant in the room instead.

I Am Sun//Taking the Moon as a Lover

I don't believe too much in revisiting old lovers

Except the moon at 3 am

I can't seem to shake that mother fucker
As I sing to Her and She sings back to me

"Gods and Goddesses
Bless those I have loved before you
Though they bent me in half
The torn tendons have brought me to this heart"

I came into this world kicking and screaming and I will be damned if you're going to shut me up for 80 years then let me go out the same way. I will make noise as long as I'm here.

All my life I thought I was a fire
A force, bold, fierce, hard to touch
I am finding now that I may be water
For I am constantly drowning in myself

Toxic Thinking

I feel like I never write when I'm happy. I only ever write when I'm sad and maybe that's the reason God made me the way He did. Maybe that's why life makes me so tired all the time. So I can fulfill His destiny for me. Maybe it's selfish to ask for something different.

I
pledge
allegiance
to

no

man

Nope, not even one. I pledge allegiance to every woman, though.

Except KellyAnne Conway
and Tomi Lahren, fuck her.

I'm always torn between being the confident,
mysterious, jaded, asshole that people can't resist

or

The sickly sweet, heart on my sleeve, give my life up
for anyone kind of person that people walk all over.

One is who I want to be.
The other is who I have always been.

All I've ever known middles.
Is there even an in between?

I feel like I'm on hold on God's emergency hotline and He hasn't gotten to my call waiting.

I am tired but I'm not hanging up yet.

Anxious

I think a lot about how Elvis died so young and Janis Joplin and Amy Winehouse and how I will probably die young and how I was not as good as I should have been even though I always wanted to be better.

When I die, I want the love that sits heavy on my bones to explode into the earth as a tangible force, suffocating everyone in delicate tenderness.

May what is inside of me always be louder, bolder, and braver than the demons.

It's true that love isn't for everybody
I just want to love my own body so badly
I want my skin to feel like a privilege, not a prison
I want to stop existing for just a couple minutes
I get the whole concept of me being the problem
If I have issues, how do I solve them?
Is it possible to be this lonely all the time?
Is wanting stability such a crime?
Maybe I had my chance and I blew it
Maybe I let it go and never knew it
Am I trapped in this loneliness?
Confined to the solitude?
Is it my voice or my looks? My heart or my attitude?
It's like I'm a tree in the woods no one's reached yet
I am uprooting and no one can hear it

How do I change internal to freeing?
How do I stop screaming "someone please love me?"

I refuse to allow bitter seasons to turn me cold.

There is an ember of warmth and love inside of me and by sheer willpower, I will not let it die.

The tips of my fingers may freeze but my heart will never.

Maybe I will never be profound
Only profane
I will be damned if I'm going to let that silence me

"Someone stole the sunshine out of my best girl!
Who did this? Bring it back, you monster!"

He screamed from the foot of the mountain

"Bring back her sunshine, please please bring it back.
You killed my best girl. I just want her to come
home."

He wept from the top

Do I sink or do I swim?
Do I fly or do I fall?

Without Limits

You can't convince people to care about you
You can, however, convince yourself
That people are worth caring about
Which is infinitely more valuable

Choose to love people
Choose to have your heart broken
A thousand more times
If that means you can pour your soul out
To a thousand more people

After every single hurt
Every letdown
Every disappointment
You can become a more tender,
More gentle version of yourself
Or you can let the pain make you calloused
Bitter, angry, and full of spite
That is a choice you will have to make on your own
You can let the heat make you harder or softer

Choose the freedom of love

[2/4]

There was no dragon. There was a young woman screaming pain and fire out of the tower window. She wasn't scary looking. She looked fragile, like one swing of a sword could take her out. As the princess took in her surroundings, she noticed that the walls were lined with anger, disappointment, rejection, and fear. Memories and painful recollections that the "dragon" had been collecting all her life. It occurred to the princess that this fortress, the breathing fire, constant roars of despair; these were nothing more than defense mechanisms to keep anyone and everyone at a safe distance - far, far away. This was not a monster. It was a twenty-four year old protecting herself from lining these walls any higher.

Things do not have to last forever
To be beautiful
They are beautiful simply because they are

Moving on is also beautiful
Choose to mourn
You must let it hurt
Then you should let it go

Next Time They Will Kiss Me First

If your hands are not full of sweet intention
Do not lay them on me
If you do not intend to follow through
Spare me the trembling hands

Please

My skin is fragile and my nerves are exposed
I am vulnerable and I will believe you

All I want is a cottage, a couple of rescue pets, a good whiskey, and a good (wo)man.

I am Woman
Made of lightning
Born of the Daughters that you burned and buried
Sculpted of their clay turned ashes

I demand that you bring me
Face to face with
Thunder
I wish to look him in the eyes
As I dethrone his heinous highness

I am stillness and fear
Crashing down from every sky
Warrior, I bear the great and powerful
Scars of all those before me
Who were slain and laid
To rest in power
Women, mothers, witches
Unwilling to accept defeat
Never bowing in their complacency
Instead rising in their glory
Bless them
For they are the stars I was built from

Bring me Thunder
I am not afraid

I was young the first time it happened to me
When I first learned to fear men
I saw a dirty magazine in a dumpster
My curiosity kicked in

Little did I know about
The man who left the magazine
Because I was looking through the pages
Behind some bushes where he found me

He said "follow me and stay quiet,"
And quiet I sure stayed
As I and the little boy I was with
Trailed this man into an alleyway

A grown man looked at us
And demanded we show each other
What my parents said we kept private
As some form of punishment or another

"We know each other, we've seen it," we said
Our little legs ready to run as fast as they can
But I suppose in a moment of guilt he said "go,"
Somehow we escaped that man

I really realize how lucky I was to be free
His zipper was already unzipped
Counting back on it now, I'm appalled
That boy was five and I was six

Shame set into us both very deep
As we vowed this was our deepest secret
I'm 24 now saying it for the first time
I'm so sorry I couldn't keep it

I was seven the second time I remember
I got violated as a kid
And maybe this man never touched me
But I'll never forget what he did

He had more power than I'll ever admit
It was an adult who was close to the family
I didn't recognize how strange it was
That this grown man watched me pee

I squashed it down for many years
Because I was lucky I was never raped
I would be lying if I told you, though
I don't have nightmares of his face

I have told two people in my whole life about it
One babysitter when I was ten
The other was my mom at twenty-two
And I never spoke of it again

The next time happened I was nineteen
It was my ex-boyfriend and I was drunk
I never filed a report or pressed charges
The evidence wasn't concrete enough

I told four people about my assault
My RA, the coordinator, a friend, and a cop
I didn't go public until I was 23
By then the timing was lost

I still have dreams where I'm writhing
Screaming "NO!" then a hand over my mouth
With tears streaming down my face to my ears
Then the memories fade in and out

I was an avid believer of victims
Before this one happened to me
Something shifts when it's you
All you hear is "well, what were you wearing?"

My story never seemed credible enough
I was drinking and no one but us knew
So in a court in front of a dozen judges
All I thought was "no one will believe you"

Men touch my shoulders and small of my back
Without my permission or consent
I brush it off and serve them beers
I should take it as a compliment

I am twenty-four now and it happens all the time
So I smile a little and flirt back a little
I asked for this because I'm a bartender
This business has no room for middles

If I get too loud I'm taking it too far
If I tell them "stop" I don't get tipped at the bar

I hate it, I hate it, I hate it, I hate it
Crawling over my skin like a thousand bugs
I feel like I don't have control over my body
Every time a strange man says "can I get a hug?"

How do I convince anyone
That I never asked for this?
When people are committed to protecting abusers?

Exodus 16:6

Screaming

"Look at all these blessings! I still love you!"

Weeping

"I don't care where you are, just come home to me"

Reaching

"Your hand. One finger. Whatever you can give me. Please."

As I drown the noise out in another drink

"I heard you were running low on inspiration
Here are some troubled waters to help you with that
Love you always,
-G "

If it feels like home
If the love is safe
You can take it back because I don't want it

I want passion and sparks and fire in our blood. I want
flames in our eyes and a touch of pure lust. I want wild
and crazy and freedom and flames. I want 3 a.m. sex
and the way you say my name. I want "baby, I love you
but I swear this is it," I want yelling and fighting and
screaming "I QUIT!" I want to miss you so badly it feels
like someone stole an organ. I want everything I do
without you to seem boring. I want the "can't get
enough of each other," kind of kisses. I want "oh look,
a shooting star," but we both know our wishes. I want
the madly in love kind of cliché. I want you wrapped
around my fingers for the rest of my days. I want to feel
lost without you in such a big world. I want to be
reminded over and over that I'm your girl.

                    If I have to worry about it
                If it becomes too much of a fight
            You can take it back because I don't want it

I want safety and security, I want routine and comfort. I
    want communication a priority so neither of us gets
    hurt. I want a home with a garden and Christmas
photos with our pets. I want "we're surprising the kids
with Disneyland," so we bought them little hats. I want
    my best friend and my ally, next to me when life gets
    hot. I want to think "how could anyone want anyone
else?" when I look at what I've got. I want the peace of
    loving you like air in my lungs. I want tiny romantic
gestures and "welcome home, baby," hugs. I want the
perfunctory kisses at bedtime and to wake up with you
by my side. I want to rest assured and never question
                that you're in this with me for life.

My heart will get every single thing she deserves
Even if I am the one to give it to her

Take that as you will

This is a love letter
To all the girls with squishy tummies and jiggly thighs

They have convinced you that you are not beautiful
For their own sake
Because ugly tries to breed ugly

They hide behind their own insecurity and hate
With the ever so popular "it's not healthy" campaign
And beg you to change

Don't let some assclown douche boy with a
backward hat, unresolved daddy issues, and a snuff
addiction tell you to lose weight to be healthy

You will never, as long as you live, be required to hate
yourself into adjusting to standards you did not
decide on

Queen mother, Hera, Aphrodite
Exist in their own curves
Nobody could tell them shit
People still worship those women
You exist in the same power, my beautiful comrades

And if you find that you are feeling
As if you walk this earth alone
That no man will respect you
Love your perfect body
Or treat you right

I will

So let me just tell you about the week I've had
You ever have one where it's so good
Then just... so bad?

I'm not much of a complainer
I normally would not have much to say here
However, I think it needs to be noted
That I have let this stop me from growing
Now that I've addressed that
I need to get back to the facing the facts

This is the point where I either let go or dive deep
Am I going to stay wading because of my fear of the
sea?
Am I in over my head? Will I let the water drown me?
Or am I the lifeguard I keep claiming to be?
This is the point where I need to either put up or shut
up
While maybe it has a little to do with what you
overcome
The mark of a true leader is getting their shit done

My problem is that I can't be a coward
While simultaneously expecting the world on a platter
I can see it happening and I can see what I'm doing
I'm not even proud of my success I'm scared of
losing it
I'm so terrified of failure I don't know how to fix it
Or even where to start
What the hell is this attitude every time I miss the
mark?

What happened to standing up tall and owning my
actions?
Who is this victim inside me with a superiority
complex?

There's no way that's me, the Sunshine, the brave
That's the coward ass demon laughing at my grave
I sometimes feel like I'm knocking at my own devil's
door screaming
"Either let her die or set her free"
Because this defeated and timid woman just isn't me

I know I have to either rise up or die trying
This middle man bullshit isn't in my personality
I came into this world loud and confident
I was taught to be bold, and smart, and handle it
I am not the sum of what I'm convinced I'm doing
wrong
That's just my pathetic excuse for not staying strong

My options became try with everything
Or let it all go
I was one finger holding on to the mental tightrope
I almost slipped

But I won't do it

My best might not always be enough
But I'll be damned if I don't try
If I go out giving it all I've got
Then what a way to die

I would rather exhaust all of my own energy
Than let someone else take me away from me

Everything I touch turns to gold
Everything I love turns to dust

Black eye bags, sunken and wet from crying. My palms are pressed flat against the granite as I stare myself in the mirror and plead

"Don't do this. Do not rip this one apart this time. What is wrong with you that you constantly have to destroy everything? Please, please, don't do this. I like this one."

A devilish laugh, narrow eyes, and the smuggest smirk that anyone has ever seen slides across the lips of the person staring back at me.

"You know who you are. Just let it happen. It will all be ashes before you know it. Now stand back sweetheart, I don't want you to get burned."

A Letter to Myself

You met me at a really weird time in my life
And you loved me at a really weird time in my life

I hope I'm brave enough to love you for the rest it

My sweetness locked eyes with my demons
    and they fell in love

My thorns were born of rain
    but oh, so were the roses

Vulnerability

I hate airports and flying
Not only because it means I'm leaving again
And I am petrified that I will never find
Somewhere that feels like home
But also because
I'm fucking terrified of dying in a plane crash
Turbulence makes me wildly uneasy
And since we're being honest here
I pretend to be a lot smarter than I am when
Airplanes don't make any sense to me
I don't understand how they work
Fear of the unknown, I guess

I hate that my life echoes my own poetry all the time
I can't tell if it's poetic irony or poetic justice
No one ever gets it and not to revert back
To being fourteen again but
On some level it makes me feel like no one gets me
I'm scared I will never meet someone whose life
Also echoes their poetry and that if I do
I will be Poe and they will be Frost
Or worse

Bukowski

When I wake up as a wildfire
Raging through my own emotional forest
I will not tell myself I am being too much
That it is time to cool down
I will burn through the deepest parts of who I am
Leaving only the stable structure underneath
And I will build from there

When I wake up as a hurricane
Washing through my heart's city
I will not ask myself to stop pouring down
As I am blowing through roofs and breaking levees
Flooding everything I know
I will wash it all away and let it drift into the ocean
And I will build from there

When I wake up as calm and steady
As the gentle summer wind
I will rejoice in the patience
I have given myself to grow
I will soak up the sunshine, I will relish in the rain
I will thank the universe for giving me a clean slate
And I will build from there

May every meltdown, may every storm
May every day where I have to battle a demon
Bring a brand new me
Humbled, I will always stay grateful
That I have disasters to help me start again

Do yourself a favor:

Have the hard talk.
It may not produce the results you want,
But tomorrow will be the beginning of the rest of
your life.

Take it or Leave It/I Will Not Hate You

I am in the business of loving people completely in whatever capacity I am capable of doing that in.

I had to teach myself that it is okay
To sleep in the middle of the bed
When I have always tried to take up just the left
Maybe one day I'll find someone to fill the right side
But as it stands right now this whole bed is mine

This is My Baggage

I procrastinate on the things I'm invested in
I guess I'm just too scared to face the rejection
I hold down relationships like a hot air balloon
One beautiful moment then it's gone too soon
And I skin myself alive for the sake of transparency
But it's becoming apparent that no one is listening to me
I say I would die for every person I've ever come across
I can't tell if I'm more afraid of if that's true or if it's not
I remind myself of my mom a lot
It's not my best trait but it's all that I've got
You wouldn't believe how many people I have abandoned
It's sick but I would rather be disgusted than feel nothing
And at the end of the day, I know I push away
Every single decent person who walks into my life
Terrified; they don't mean to hurt me, but they might
As it turns out, I am a coward
No matter how much "bravery" I falsely put forward

I don't know what scares me more
The idea that nobody will ever be in love with me
Or the idea that somebody will

I guess it's not fun when it's not a chase anymore
And I guess that I'd rather be challenged than adored
Maybe I get turned on by back and forth feelings
Maybe I secretly like it when emotions are fleeting
Can somebody tell me what the fuck that's all about?
I'm caught in this maze, just trying to get out
I get the concept of getting in control of my own life
But if this is what it is I don't want it, alright?
I don't want to keep playing games and fucking around
What is it like to have my emotional feet on solid ground?

Some habits are hard to break
This habit might break me

"Why do you have to do this so often to feel real?"

A small voice inside her asked

"I do this because I feel too real normally, pal"

She said back, casually

I remember being drunk one night
Crying "I just want to sit at Jesus' feet"
That's the closest in a while
I've been to the real me
See, the reason that Jesus gave us grace
Wasn't for us to just spit in God's face
I know that here in the midst of rebellion
I knew that when I first fell in love with Him
It's a vicious cycle I got myself in
I want to break out but I don't know where to begin
It's almost easier being stuck
Than it would be to pull myself out of the mud
I wrestle and wrestle and fight and fight
Honestly, without Him, I just get so tired
It's not even about my sin anymore
It's that I can't hear His voice anymore
It's that I don't feel His heart anymore
It's that I don't care enough to try anymore
I blame it on the heartbreak, the bad times, the hurt
I do that because I can't make things any worse
And honestly, it's all just a petty excuse
Because it hurts to look in the mirror
And tell myself "it's you"
I'm the one who stopped seeking
I'm the one who divided
Right now, in this moment, I am far away from Him
I know that at 2:05 am
I don't know where I'm at but I know where He is
On the other side of this spiritual bridge
That I've been building because someone burned me
But that doesn't negate that He is Holy
That He is keeping this bridge from burning
That He is on the other side waiting
That I will come home eventually
......Will I?

I became free

The day I started believing
That some of what happened
Was my fault

These last few months have just been us driving around to the sound of static radio. The truth is, we stopped making memories a long time ago but we found comfort in sitting on the same respective sides of the car we always have. We were not in love anymore. Not with each other, at least. That reality burned worse than the rum we used to spend nights drinking; it is more bitter than the taste your kiss leaves on my lips now. Maybe we stayed together because we fell into wistfulness about a future we might have been grown up enough to have. In all of those wine-drunk we spent nights staying up making promises, we never took into account the respective directions our lives were leading us. We made plans over bonfires and clung to the hope that love was enough to sustain it. Neither of us seems to be able to stomach the obviousness that our flames have turned to embers and it's just a matter of time before there's nothing but ashes. Even though you've been riding passenger seat for a while, our souls said goodbye after the summer turned to fall when the air was still warm. It is no one's fault that our love shifted with the seasons. As we drive now up against the icy mountainside and I do not reach for your hand, I realize we have grown as cold as my fingertips. I will have to turn this car around soon.

- Do you remember when that used to be us?

Something about this wind feels warm
It feels secure and smells like a different time
Something about this scene feels familiar
The swampy air, roads lined with trees
But I just don't think this is the place for me
(This is not my home)
Something about these people's smiles
The way they walk and talk
Their southern drawls
The jazz music that fills the air
Reminds me this small world is theirs
It turns out that the Big Easy
Just wasn't the place for me
(This is not my home)
Baton Rouge, Lafayette, Hammond, Houma
I keep causing trouble wherever I go now
I'm chasing pavements here and so
It's time now to hit the road
Try as I might, whoever I may be
This just isn't the place for me
(This is not my home)

I am the human embodiment
of one (1) good
tinder date
before
you never talk again

Listen to me.

Let them say what they are going to say
Let their lies and their hate drip off their tongue like
venom
Let them spit your name out of their mouth like a
sour cherry
They will speak their cruelty
They will try to tear you down limb by limb
Demolish your reputation little by little
Let them

Do not retaliate
You are not required to tear them down
The way they tore you down
You do not need to hurt them back
Choose to be the side of love
Choose not to look down on those who slander you
Instead, keep your own eyes forward
And combat their loathing with sincere sweetness
Working your ass off
Proving them wrong

Do not let the pain or anger take you down the
darkest road
Because once you've lost your heart you have lost it
all

[3/4]

Nothing could have prepared the armored princess for what happened next. Her highness removed the ironclad helmet and let it clang to the ground next to her. The dragon heard the noise, stopped in her tracks, and cautiously, slowly even, turned to look at the princess face to face for the very first time.

All I Ever Make

I keep a collection of my broken things
Gripped tightly in my palms and between my fingers

I've been trying to will them back into wholeness,
Love their pieces back together but
I'm running out of space because my hands are small
Just like my father's

I don't know how to drop the broken things
I'm worried that I would just create more destruction
That I may drop myself, too

Two versions of me sitting on opposite sides of a
boxing ring.

One fighting for her heart.

The other for her autonomy.

Angry, jaded, the first one speaks,

"How can you put yourself out there when you
are bound to get hurt? Why don't we just protect
ourself instead? Let good things come to us?"

The second stands, tightening her gloves, moving to
the middle of the ring.

"Everyone already has that mentality, you coward!
Being bold means that we will be shot down 99
times instead of 100. I am asking you to let me be
bold. It is going to hurt sometimes but the pain
makes us real. The outcome is only as bad as you
allow it to be."

Tender, timid, letting down her fists, the first
whispers "I don't know if I can survive it again,"
her voice crumbles.

"Maybe not, but what a way to go out," the
second says, pulling her into her arms.

I pray that we learn together to let our
embarrassments humble us instead of anger us

People told me all the time growing up
That life is not a fairytale

I'm finding more and more that it is
I have just been searching for the wrong plots

I Hear Heaven/Hell is How People Remember You

I just want to leave a legacy

Whether it's my love story
A grand discovery
Nurturing the world into healing
Or fighting for those who can't fight for themselves
Until it kills me

I refuse to leave this place without making it better
than I found it

One Day I Will be Stronger

I talk an awful lot of shit about knowing my worth for someone who keeps seeking her value in other people.

What does it say about me that I can be built and
broken so easily?

I haven't showered in four days
Last night I had cashews and hot Cheetos for dinner
I still smile at strangers on the street
They always say "hey, how are you doing?"
And I say "good! How are you?" back to them
But I'm not good, am I?
Not when my emotions have been all over the place
When I'm brushing my teeth but not washing my face
I've had the same drawn on eyebrows for days and
they look terrible
I think my cat can tell I'm only half there when I feed
her in the morning
Because I'm not cooing at her like I normally do
And I'm crying on the Lyft ride home
And everything irritates me
I keep telling myself I want to go shopping for
clothes but what for?
I'm just going to lay in bed in my underwear all day
I have all the ingredients to make curry but I order
out anyway
"At least you're eating," I tell myself
But I know better
It's the end of fall now and the sunflowers are dying

Am I dying too?

You'd think for someone
    Who wants to be liked so badly
        I would do a better job
            Of getting people to like me

Dane County Regional Airport

Maybe one day I will start flying toward things instead of away from them.

"Why are you so obsessed with the stars?"

"That is what my bones are made of. The stars are my creation.

Take me home, take me home, take me home."

The Pot and the Kiln

Know that I absolutely had to falter
I had to crumble and break
I had to turn to complete ashes
To get here

This last year was so hard
That it would be easy
To look at the girl I was and say
"She's dead. That girl is dead."
Examining it now
I see she's not dead at all

She is a lightning bolt of a woman
Fierce, fearless, bold
She is a breeze on a hot summer day
Gentle, forgiving, free

People commented on how strong I was
I wasn't strong, though
Strength is allowing yourself to feel what's wrong
Instead of constantly patching things together

Strength is not always knowing the answer
Admitting you were wrong
I was not strong just for holding myself up
Because I went crashing, tumbling down
In a catastrophic collision with reality
When I lost myself completely

Then I came face to face
With the most raw
Extraordinarily executed
Version of me

I know now that my strength
Comes from my tenderness
From looking hate in the face and saying
"I will not retaliate
I love you far too much
I will not strike back"

Life, love, fear, sadness
Blowing through me like bullet holes
Was the only way I was ever going to become
The kindness I am now

The fire wasn't killing me
It was creating me
To it I owe my life

What's coming will come
What's going will go
Be not afraid of how hard the wind blows
Be excited about the direction it carries you

Newton's 3rd Law of Motion

I will have a hundred more downfalls
And a hundred and one more redemptions

and here I am, happy,
in spite it of and because of it

[4/4]

It turns out that the dragon and the princess were the
same person

and she rescued herself.

[1 LEO IS TYPING…]

VIRGO

The saddest truth of it all
Is that friends can sometimes break your heart too

You are not bound by the shackles and chains you
have assigned to yourself.

The world is harsh and cruel sometimes but
you, dear one, are not. You are (now and as long as
I've known you) pure selflessness and loyalty. Do not
let them steal that from you. I know it all seems so
hard right now. I do not know what you are feeling
inside. I do not know the darkness and loneliness that
you are possibly suffering. I do know, though, that I
have felt dark and lonely. I know how it feels to have
people hate you and try to destroy you for something
you cannot change. I understand that you are feeling
like your limbs belong to someone else's trees. It is
hard to believe that life will get better, easier, that one
day you might feel like you fit into your own skin. I
promise, I swear to you, that one day you will.

Let me tell you, sweet friend, you are not
their narrow beliefs of what you should be. You do
not belong to their mindsets. You are not required
to behave in a way that is pleasing to them. You
have one life here and you are entitled to spend it
living in your own authenticity. They do not have
the power to take that from you.

Your truth has always been kindness. You have
always been good to me even when others were not.
When I had no one else to depend on you stood by

my selfish side even though you had your own demons to battle. There is nothing in this world I can extend to you to thank you for that.

You have always believed yourself to be thorns but you are the stem. Sturdy and strong, unwilling to stand down. Right now it feels like you are walking through a dark alley blindfolded, searching for who you are. I can not remove the mask from your eyes but I am behind you fighting off enemies the very best I can. I am with you until you open the right door. I will not let the cruelty take you. I will spend any amount of time and energy battling with you for your autonomy.

Please know that as long as I am alive you will find safety and truth in that. I see your life changing all around you and I promise I will be patient with you. I promise that even if you are far away you are close to me. Be it one day, one month, one year since we have last talked, I am on your side. Your world is wonderful. Your heart is beautiful. You are a person whom I respect and adore, whose personhood is valuable and useful. You are one of the very reasons I still believe in the beauty of mankind. You make a difference here.

[1/2 VIRGOS HAS LEFT THE CHAT]
[1/2 VIRGOS IS IN THE LOBBY]

LIBRA

A Field of Sunflowers

I am listening to the rainfall
Through an open window
I am missing you like hell today
Because before you
I never even liked the rain
So now it kind of sounds like nostalgia

It has been years since we fell in love
But I can still hear a future we never had
In every single drop

You taught me what rain means
It is a kiss from the sky to the earth
It brings nourishment for things to grow
My oh my, how my love still grows
Even if you never feel the same way again

When I was younger than I am now
I only ever saw gray skies and inconvenience
When it was always the weather
We could wrap up in together
If we had ever gotten the chance

Like the rain is sometimes short
So was our ever fleeting love
I still remember though - I still remember

The way rain sometimes brings a hurricane
The way the rain gives sunflowers water to grow
I know you did the same for me

As the flood of us came washing in
As the drought of you leaving swept me away
I appreciate the rain more these days
I appreciate the sun more these days

If you're ever curious, in case you ever want to know
Our love, your heart, came with many seeds
One for every time you have crossed my mind
In the last five years
The garden in this field is endless
Tours are free any time you want to see
What all those showers bloomed in me

Your name used to sound like
An echo on the walls of forever
Now it just sounds like
Whispers of a past I kissed goodbye already

Reckless Idealist

This river wild runs wide and deep
Past selves for whom I'd lost my peace
These days it is with ease I sleep
Love has not given up on me

The pain that brought me to my knees
Proved a chance to wash people's feet
Servanthood has made me see
Love has not given up on me

It's in the air, at night it creeps
It waits as calm as a steady sea
To bless me with a soul to keep
Love has not given up on me

For a time I thought love left when we
Blew away with the autumn leaves
Wind still swayed through those old palm trees
Love has not given up on me

After the tides rolled in and set me free
Serenity washed over in a cloud of dreams
I hear it humming, to me it pleads
"Dear one, please don't give up on me"

I am not some specialty wine
Sitting on your kitchen counter collecting dust
That you're saving for the right time

I am the whole vine of grapes
That the wine is born from
I am the vineyard tour
That people buy vacation packages to
I am the water from the sky
The heat from the sun
That raises the harvest

I deserve better than a shelf

Have you moved on but not let me know?
I've learned to move forward without letting go
Can I move on and love someone new?
Under her, not over you

If there's any chance you might love me again
You have to let me know so I can let this thing end
He deserves to know the truth
That I am
Under him, not over you

Picture this: I'm ten years old
I dream of love
How it unfolds
I dream of holding hands
I dream of weddings
Of romantic stares
Of happy endings
I have no idea
What I'm in for yet
Because the love I find
Is as good as it gets

Picture this: I'm seventeen
You're twenty-one
It's oh so fleeting
We never say it
Not to each other
Because you got scared
And ran for cover
I was hurt
I missed you so
I wasn't ready
To let you go
The timing was terrible
We were too young
To know what to do
With that kind of love

Picture this: I'm twenty-three
I'm learning now
How to be me
I take some trips
I see some sights
I sleep alone
Under God's bright lights
I see mountains and beaches
I see shores and coasts
The one thing I don't see
Is thing I want to see most
But it's been years
And we don't talk
A part of me with you
Is always lost

Picture this: I'm thirty-five
I have some kids
I'm a great wife
I'm happy now
I feel fulfilled
In the back of my mind
I wonder still
What you're doing
On these cold nights
Because in September
You'll be thirty-nine
It's been ten years
Since I sent you "hey
I just wanted to say
Happy birthday"
And when my teenagers ask me
To tell them about love
I talk about their father
Not about us

Picture this: I'm 50 now
My children have grown
And they've all moved out
I have an ex-husband
We just grew apart
He told me he knew
He never had my heart
So I go out and try things
Like antiquing and thrifting
I can't help but wish
That you were here with me
When I was young I thought
That we'd be doing this together
Timing's a bitch
But still I remember
On my way home
I pick up some eye cream
I browse the magazine section
And check out a few things
It's on this summer night
With a book in my hand
On a chair on my lawn
I wonder where you're at

Picture this: I'm getting old
Or so I feel
So I've been told
My hair is gray
My hands, they shake
I live alone
On my estate
I'm on my porch
The air is warm
I think of you
A smile forms
Rocking chair thoughts of
How young I was
And try as you might
You don't outgrow love
I lived a great life
I reached all of my plans
Well, all but one
I never got to your hands
I don't have much time
Or much else to do
But on the other side
I see you
So I walk through the doors
To that pearly gate
No matter how long it took
I knew this was fate

10/4 - Loud and Clear

This is either our ultimate hello
Or our final goodbye
I am not willing to spend any more of
My few years on earth
In limbo with you

I have decided today that sweet and bold
Are not a dichotomy
I will be sweet for you forever
But I am bold enough to make this decision

I destroy everything at the beginning
Before it has the chance to start
I'm more afraid of falling in love
Than I am of a broken heart

That's why I do ridiculous things
Like ask if you even want to do this anymore
I pretend that I'm giving you an out
When it's really my emergency exit door

Then I play the victim
Like I didn't just tear myself open
It's way easier to do that, it seems
Than admit that I might be broken

You should know I always knew what I was doing
I just made you the one to do it
I would much rather be the hurting damsel
Than admit I'm the one who blew it

Right Person, Wrong Universe

Please understand that I am not angry with you
This was not your choice

There are more galaxies
Than can be named or numbered
I know that I have an infinite amount
Of lifetimes and dimensions
To get to love you

This wasn't the right one

There is an 18-year-old made of fire
Mourning that you don't talk to her anymore
And there is a 24-year-old built of peace
Rejoicing that she ever got to know you at all

Maybe a snow-covered cabin on a mountain was
never in the cards for us, but we got to fall in love,
which now that I'm older seems like enough

There have been so many sunrises
And so many sunsets
Here on this island I've built for myself
As I take in the sights and feel the love all around me
I'm finding that I am comfortable in my own skin

I hope you find everything you're looking for

I hope life finds you in the crazy
ravishes you with beauty
blinds you with magnificence
steals you from your sorrow

I hope grace meets you in your mess
gifts you with hope
allows you the space to grow
shows you the world isn't so bad

I hope love frees you from the chains
showers you with freedom
caresses you with tenderness
holds you close and protects you

I hope life finds you
I hope grace meets you
I hope love frees you

I love you forever my friend

I'm not implying that you will need it
But if you ever do
My light is still yours to sit in

[1/2 LIBRAS HAS LEFT THE CHAT]
[1/2 LIBRAS IS IN THE LOBBY]

SCORPIO

Somebody else will get the quips
Sarcasm and sweetness
Somebody else will appreciate the hell
Out of my special interests and fierce loyalty
Somebody else will do long distance
Or hard circumstances

Somebody else will love me the right way

Always in a crowded room
My eyes were hoping to find you
From everyone else's point of view
Yours were searching for mine, too

Only they weren't

You never wanted me
You were looking for new eyes to meet

I wrote this while i was Healing, Only i don't know if i have:

my baby, Please know i didn't want things to End So Horribly, or Ever at all.

We just did not have what it takes to maintain A functional relationship So soon.

i need you to know i tried With all of me to Overcome the issues within me, within us

but Reality has a way of showing me how even when i plan Things, i cannot Hope for anything other than what fate has decided. this Is all probably for The best.

I would have you and lose you all over again to learn
what I learned from you

You flakey, selfish, asshole.

I sometimes wish someone would jump to my honor
and defend me
I want someone to tell you

"That girl did not deserve what you did to her
You cracked a hole in a someone made of sunshine
I would never do that
She deserved to be loved wholly
But you only ever loved her selfishly
Which is not love at all
That girl is made of peace
You took a piece out of her
But she is a fighter
So right now instead of grieving what you did
She is picking up crumbs, trying to collect enough
To replace what you took
So that she can love others even harder
You only ever saw her for what she is not
You wanted her to change for you
Instead of you stepping up and being someone
Who is deserving of the absolute flood of love she is

She loved you in spite of it
I am angry that you got to her before I did
Because to me she is golden
She is selfless patience and kind-hearted goodness
She is bright and brilliant
Every single atom of her is made of love
I would have never given love a bad name
The way you did
I would never have flooded her head with doubts

I am in love with her, I mean it when I say it
It is not some filler word to appease her
Like it was with you
I would cross canyons and gorges
To get her what she deserves
You wouldn't even forsake your own selfish desires
To get her the bare minimum
If there was one cup of water left on the planet
And she was on fire
You would drink it because you were thirsty
But if you were on fire and she had no water at all
She would have bled herself dry
Trying to put out your flames
And you never deserved that
You never deserved her"

No one has done that yet
And maybe no one ever will silently curse you
While loving me the right way

So this is me telling you myself:
I deserved better

You stole the fire from inside of me with your bare hands and used it to ignite your own ego. I never stood a chance.

I came to you as a match; ready to light up your world

You came to me as a tsunami; ready to wreck me

I do not need to be cruel to you
Revenge is not my heart's desire
There is no punishment greater than
That you will never have me again

I collapsed myself underneath you
Because you demanded that I let my walls down
So I did, with every single empty kiss
I collapsed myself underneath you
Under your touch, under your misguided direction
Because you made me believe you knew me
Better than I knew me
I collapsed myself underneath you
Until I was a heaping pile of clay for you to mold
But I was never quite malleable enough so
I collapsed myself underneath you
To give you a reason to stay, to tell me the truth
But you wouldn't
Even after you have gone and
I am the pile of ashes you burned me to
I collapse myself into the thought of you
How I could be so stupid as to allow you to do this
You see, you did not break my heart
You broke me in half
Stripped of who I used to be
That girl is a ghost of a figure that is still
Collapsed underneath you

I had a dream last night
Where you were crying in your car
Like you did that one time
Outside of the Halloween store
Back when we were first falling
In this dream
You said to me
"Baby, baby, baby
I can't do this without you
You were my best friend and I made a mistake
I got us a place
So I never have to go another day
Without kissing your face
And I'm so sorry it took this for me to see it
But I love you and I mean it
Please come home to me
My bed feels so empty
Baby, baby, baby"
And you sobbed into your hands
I fell apart into my own
Not because I want you back
But because I wasn't strong enough
To say no

I Think I Finally Shed You

That red shirt I left at your house
The one I demanded that you give back
In a fit of rage, when I still had no idea
How badly you really fucked me up

I used to breathe it in deep
Every night before bed
Because it smelled like you
Like your home

I picked it up for the first time
Since those lonely nights
And I sobbed, I wept the biggest tears I ever have
Not because it smelled like you still
But because it smelled like me

A Letter to a Scorpio

I can no longer write of my sadness
Of what you did, of how you burned me
Without admitting some of this was my fault
The absolute truth of it
Is that I hurt you too
I am not naive and I am no longer
Too clouded by my own stab wound
To acknowledge that it was a knife fight
I am sorry I did not
Accept defeat more gracefully

I relish the sweet memories
While thanking you for the time
For the secrets, for the new interests
I am grateful to you for being
A catalyst of growth I have never known

This Leo is no longer bitter
I am sending you love

For This I am Thankful

You gave me a hot hammer to the heart
In return
The universe gave me a glue gun

I was shattered
Now I am a mosaic

[LEO HAS BLOCKED THIS USER]

SAGITTARIUS

If I could go back and undo any series of time, if I could string together any chain of events to create one possible outcome, I would have been there. I let us both down.

(1) Jesus Was A Radical Brown Man

Like you understand that Jesus, our Christ/ Savior/King of all Kings, was a peaceful brown Jewish man from the Middle East, right? If He came here needing shelter y'all would deny Him and call Him a terrorist. If He came here trying to work and spread the good news of His arrival, y'all would tell Him to go back to His country and swear He's stealing jobs and raping people. You understand that when He got mad about how we're treating people of color and started calling you out on that crappy behavior you would call Him a libtard and a snowflake while harassing Him? Like, y'all FULLY understand that right? You cannot simultaneously preach "make America great again" and worship a radical brown man for dying for our sins on the same Sunday. You chose someone to worship already.

(2) Thank You, Dr. Blasey Ford

This is not an "agree to disagree" situation. This is a "you start believing womxn and other survivors or you can exit my life. If you do not believe them you do not believe me. You will change your mind or you will lose me," situation. This isn't politics anymore. This has nothing to do with liberals or conservatives anymore. This is about you wanting to push your hateful agenda through so badly that you are willing to let us get raped and sexually assaulted to achieve it. This is about me thinking outside of myself and being part of a new narrative for women.

On the days when I am frail and weak
My grandma speaks to me
She says "when you were tiny and brand new
I prayed that The Lord make use of you
And seeing now how you have grown
I've have seen His glory shown
You are brave and bold; valiant
My tiny angel heaven sent
You've grown into who I prayed you'd be"
Is what my grandma speaks to me

On days when I am just so busy
My grandma speaks to me
She says "my sweet girl when you were little
I prayed that The Lord would make you gentle
And seeing now how you love others
Oh, His glory has been uncovered
I never doubted He loved you so
I prayed from your head down to your toes
And The Lord, how good is He?"
Is what my grandma speaks to me

On days when I am sad and miss her
My grandma speaks to me
She says "you were once just a tiny baby
Who has now grown into a woman
I am watching you and all your siblings
From my room here up in heaven
And tell your mama she's doing alright
That I listen when she talks at night
Know this, my strong little girl
I prayed that you would be of use to the world
When you were just a teeny thing
I lifted you up to the King of Kings

I said 'Father, I know you have many plans
Please always keep her safe in Your hands
She is strong willed I can already tell
And some day she may just go through hell
I am praying sweet Jesus you keep this one with you
That she love people fiercely through every issue
And that if she does not start out gentle natured
That You mold her into a peace maker'
His promises He always keeps"
Is what my grandma speaks to me

[2/2 SAGITTARIUS' DESERVED BETTER]

CAPRICORN

I Hope I Marry a Writer

I am a writer who fell for a writer and honestly that's like lighting a match in a gasoline factory. A writer who painted dreams inside of my heart, bright colors with burning intensity. Whose words were dancers doing pirouettes in my brain. Whose passion for literature came out of every single word they spoke. It sparked fireworks in my blood. It was just like that - explosion, combustion. Someone who was invested in me the same way people get invested in a story: while it lasted. All in, absorbing every single moment, every breath and sound and movement as long as I laid love down.

Listen to me. If you're going to fall for a lit major, understand that you have no clue what you're getting yourself into. You never will. The thrill of it is worth every single second.

I remember waking up that morning and I smirked because I had a dream about your crooked teeth and wicked smile. I woke up with the sound of your voice pounding loud in my head and all I could think was

"I'm going to remember you for the rest of my life. You got exactly what you wanted."

Queen

You gave me the courage to find the person I am right now. You were always a storybook character. I've always loved to read. I always wanted to be the hero. I guess you were mine.

Language lovers are flirts. They flirt with commitment, flirt with people, flirt with the idea of love. Just like words leave as soon as your lips have spilled them, lit lovers leave as soon as the second passes.

You can not ask a language lover to love you. They have chosen a lover. You are just a beautiful representation of whatever they want at that moment. Words are selfish. Words are temporary.

Baby

"Can I ask you something?"
"Always, of course."
"Please don't stop calling me that until you hate me."

Your birthday is on Christmas
And I was cruel to you
I hope you know it was not because I did not like you
It was because I did
I should have never led you on

I change my mind just as quick as I decide

[2/2 CAPRICORNS ARE IN THE LOBBY]

AQUARIUS

I Forgive You

I understand now
I forgive you
I'm sorry I made it such a fight

I am floating in an ocean of broken hearts
Drowning in a sea of friends I have lost
That do not love me anymore

[1/1 AQUARIUS WAS JUST DOING HER JOB]

PISCES

I cried the first time
I heard your laugh over the phone
Because I was in a relationship
And I just wanted to spend forever making you laugh

Last night I had a dream
About a decorated Christmas tree
All the things we could be
Hanging ornaments, you and me

I loved you in this dream, you see
Stolen kisses and a mounted wreath
By the fire drinking tea
Every Christmas, you and me

Falling into you was the easiest process
Every word, every moment, every movement
Was more natural than I have ever experienced

We have everything against us
I have never been more willing to stand against it

You felt right to me even when the world was
screaming

W

    R

        O

          N

            G

Do you have any idea what you do to me
When my head is filled with anxiety?
You are always patient and good and kind
When I ask what's on your mind a thousand times
And when I ask if you're upset ten times in a row
You mean it every time you tell me "nope"
I have never known such ease
Please please please stick around

"Go to Bed, Stormy"

When I am a crumbled panicked mess I say to you
"I'm sorry I'm sorry I'm sorry
I'm a storm
I have always been a storm
All I know is destruction and tragedy
You don't have to deal with this
You can go if you want."

You say back to me, peace in your eyes
"My beautiful, kind girl
Do not let them make you believe
That your category five hurricane of a soul
Is not absolute power
You are beautiful to me
Because you can carry people away
Sweep them off of their feet
You are a sheer force of magnificence
You do everything you do
In a big, beautiful, way or not at all
Do not let anyone tell you to dim that
Do not let anyone tell you
You should not be dealt with
You demand to be seen and felt
And that's exactly what I intend to do
Because after every tragedy
Something bigger and more beautiful is born
And I sleep best on stormy nights"

Our ship sailed onto your seas
Which I think is for the best
Because I would have set it on fire anyway

I never wanted to
I just kind of have this habit
Of taking people I might love
Crumbling the relationship in my hands
Sprinkling the ashes everywhere
Promptly complaining about the mess
Then wondering where my heart has gone

Even though it hurt like hell
While you were doing it
You shook that out of me

I am grateful to you now, seven months later
For being kind
Whoever I love next will get a better version of me
I will love them
With no projection or hard expectations
As if we are building framed pictures lining a hallway
Instead of faded polaroids in a shoebox
From a time with expiration dates

Of all the things that burned me
In that season of my life where
I was losing everything, everyone
Even myself
The two things that burned the worst were
That Costco tequila
And letting you go
I didn't want to, I hope you know
I was just too weak to fight for you

I woke up on February 26th
To a crack of thunder so loud
It shook my whole house
I gasped myself awake
At 3:08 so incoherent that
It took me ten minutes to realize
The shuddering thunder
Was the earth telling me it heard me
Saying "happy birthday to you
Wherever you are
In whatever you are doing
I wish you love"
I heard the earth loud and clear
Echo my sorrow back to me
It's your birthday today but
The storm washed away
My right to celebrate with you
Still I hope-
I hope you heard the thunder

"Don't talk about me like I'm past tense yet," you said to me.
But you always were, weren't you?
You were past tense before we ever kissed in your car.
You were past tense before you stopped responding to my messages.
You were past tense before it took all I had in me to let go of you in one day.
I loved you as a past tense since the beginning.
I always wanted to love you.
I bet I probably could have.
But it was never present.
You were never present.

Yes, I miss you
The way the waves miss the shore
The way the night sky misses the morning sun
The anguish that has been written about
A thousand times
In a thousand poems
A thousand books

Yes, I miss you
All ~~137~~ 376 days you have been gone
And you may not understand the overwhelming
Absence I feel without you
But I am positive that you will never understand
The utter destitution
I felt without me

Yes, I miss you
I also know that you missed out
This is a beautiful heart I have grown into
A beautiful life that I have come used to
I will not give you the opportunity to come and go
again
A condition of getting to love me now
Is that whoever I give this blessing to
Should be someone I trust to help me up from a dirty
floor
Dust me off and send me along
Not someone who will simply avert their eyes
At the same time, please know
I do not blame you for that
For choosing what you did
I didn't stay either
The choice was always yours
Were these not my skin and bones
I may not have come back

Yes, I miss you
My Pisces friend, my heart packed into 5 feet of pure
Unwillingness to be stepped on or trampled over
Heart of gold, kind blue eyes,
Never choosing to be a lover or a fighter
You are both to the core of you
Sweetness and sass, sarcasm and sincerity
One of the easiest things I have ever given myself to
You have no idea how many messages
I have written but not sent
The timing has never been right
When every single thing about you was easy for me
But nothing about me was easy for you
I'm okay with that

However, I am not interested in trying to maintain a
relationship with anyone
Who can watch me suffer and break
Who can see me fall apart and crash and crumble
Someone who can see that my heart is broken
And instead of offering me a hand
Offers me a silent goodbye
Slipping into the frosty winter air
Swimming away into the deep blue

I had to choose
Between fighting for me
And fighting for you

So yes, I miss you
Heart-wrenching,
Gut-wrenching,
Depths of my soul - I miss you

But I missed me more

I Also Don't Hold You Against Me

I used to tell you all the time
That I will not let bitterness break me
That I will not let cruelty make me unkind
That I won't allow the crushing weight of sadness to
Steal the love I have to give out

So I need you to know that I do not despise you
I do not hate you for having to go
I am not angry or bitter with you
I do not blame you or chastise you
I do not hate you
I understand that you had your own demons

I do not hold you against you

B N B

I want you to know
The tunnel to my heart is still in tact
If you want to walk back into me
You are still shiny and new

[1/1 LEO HAS LET GO]

ABOUT THE AUTHOR

Interests include: Astrology, outer space, Stevie Nicks, Fleetwood Mac as a second only to her aforementioned queen, Kate McKinnon, SNL as a second only to her aforementioned wife, Florence and the Machine, locating every good planetarium in the country, binge watching new television series every week once she finishes the last one too quickly, watching YouTube tutorials on beekeeping, Old Fashioneds (whiskey in general,) rescue animals, rescue children, liberal politics (ride for RBG,) podcasts, Kelly Clarkson as a 16 year old tradition, being bisexual but only liking .01% of men, seeking fulfillment via quitting jobs, constantly moving around the country for no good/obvious reason, transparency in commitment issues, SO MUCH cheese, burgers and pizza and the ensuing body positivity that must happen as a result of the burgers and pizza, constantly turning read receipts on and off at will, responding to emails but not text messages, self-improvement (but only on HER TERMS,) pumpkin pies, writing books no one will read, doing undergrad English research papers on the benefits of masturbation, talking not only ABOUT herself but TO herself, speaking absolute gibberish to her cat, being a casual witch/goth dad, taking any and all criticism very personally, curry in all of its forms, board games, Christmas music, and true crime.

Oh, she lives in Seattle with her cat, Honey. Her favorite Taylor Swift album is 1989. Or Red. She can't decide.

Made in the USA
Coppell, TX
18 May 2020